ABOUT THE AUTHOR

A multi slam winner and runner up in the 2020 UK Slam! **Jemima Hughes** hurried onto the Birmingham poetry scene in March 2017 and swiftly hurried off again after showcasing five minutes of her ongoing mental health battle.

Previously an international trampolinist and coach, Jemima strove to always support her participants emotionally as much as competitively. As reality hit that she was in need of support herself, she stepped away from her sport and lifelong passion to focus on her mental health.

During her most conflicted days she turned to writing poetry to express herself at a time when her verbal communication was minimal, consequently finding a new passion.

These days, Jemima has found her voice again, mastered timing and rhythm, and has travelled across the UK and Ireland to headline countless spoken word events. With the belief that letting someone feel heard can save a life, she's grateful to everyone who has allowed her to feel heard throughout this journey.

Website: https://www.jemimahughespoet.co.uk/
Instagram: @jemima_unspoken
Twitter: @jemima_unspoken

Jemima as a performer...

"Storm Jemima is a surge of intensity gathering on your horizon. It is a tumbling of sentiments and sincerity of message, getting harder to ignore, always ready to drop. Nothing looks quite the same after it hits." - Jasmine Gardosi.

"One of the most extraordinarily talented performers I have had the pleasure of seeing." - Clive Oseman.

"Jemima Hughes is an exciting, up and coming writer and performer whose work is as fiery as it is tender, inspiring in her ability to hold an audience safely whilst exploring subject matters that make your insides tingle and writhe with relatability. Her transparency is moving and admirable. The rhythm and musicality of her words are present on both page and stage, each word rooting its own place and significance, each adding depth to the stories she tells of journeys; of vulnerability; of fear and bravery, and most of all, of resilience. Jemima has already made huge leaps in her career and will only continue to thrive. But for me, she is still tea, warm winter fire and cosy chit chats at her core." - Nafeesa Hamid.

"Jemima is a tour de force when it comes to spoken word poetry. She pulls no punches and is brutal yet beautiful in equal measure. Now she's brought her work to the page. Treat yourselves. Read this collection and catch her live if you can." - Giovanni "Spoz" Esposito.

"If you have ever seen a choir of fireworks set to spinning wheels illuminate a night sky and observed new alphabets emerging from a flurry of shadows and sparks, then I say you are close. Dancing a personal and relatable modern narrative of light and dark, Jemima is a convincing and courageous modern storyteller." - Paul Point.

Jemima Hughes
Unorthodox

VERVE
POETRY PRESS
BIRMINGHAM

PUBLISHED BY VERVE POETRY PRESS
https://vervepoetrypress.com
mail@vervepoetrypress.com

FIRST PUBLISHED JULY 2020

Printed and bound in the UK
by ImprintDigital, Exeter

ISBN: 978-1-912565-38-2

Cover photo credit: Tim Horgan

This book is dedicated to you, Mum and Dad. You married in a storm so you know how beautiful the aftermath can be. Thank you for weathering this one so courageously. And to you, Timothy, for having faith in me when I couldn't. I never knew our kind of love existed and now I can't imagine existing without it.

Thank you Nanna for your endless encouragement. Thank you Chris, Matt and Rick for all of those hugs strong enough to hold me together. Thank you to my girls Lisa, Paige, Laura, Stevie, Jade and Aimee for treating me like nothing was wrong when nothing was right.

Most of all this book is for you. Yes you. I hope that reading it will help you in some of the ways that writing it helped me.

CONTENTS

Unorthodox

My Morphine #1

Writing through the pain
as my tears touch the page.

They blur the ink
like the line between friendship and fate.

But it's worth it
because you've probably felt the same.

Have you?

Tornado

The National Weather Service has issued a severe weather warning. Storm Jemima has hit the south.

A tornado, intensity warning F3, is set to tear through your life, turn everything on its head, emotions will be rife, this weather warning is most certainly a code red.

We cannot yet say whether the damage will be widespread
but there is sure to be a blustery path ahead.

Her sudden appearance may cause confusion,
no need to adjust, she won't be a long-lasting intrusion.
However, after the initial luminosity you may become disillusioned.

Prepare to feel a surge of adrenaline
awaken your every sense
with her first presence.
Try not to be tense.
Remember she doesn't mean to cause offence.
She is as natural as mountains or the moon's mere existence,
but with natural follows disaster,
don't fall victim to her false pretence.

With the commotion
you may want to tighten your grasp on common sense
before your thoughts condense
to only you and her,
you don't have time to build a wall for defence,
her deep rumbling is echoing,
she's hungry for you,
it's about to commence.

The lights may be out for some time.
The only electricity will be the power drawing her closer to you,
until then, enjoy the view?

A change in atmosphere right on cue,
pressure is low,
she expects nothing from you.

You're going to bind in a whirlwind of heart-pounding excitement
and fear of devastation,
please beware of her irresistible fixation
on you.
She will cling to you,
she will consume you,
she will rip off your roof leaving you exposed to who knows who

because she believes it could be good for you,
opening up to places you never knew existed.

Her judgement may be twisted
but her mystery can't be resisted,
her patterns can't be predicted,
her actions can't be restricted.

She's going to sweep you off your feet,
let you swirl amongst her cloud of frozen memories.

You being at the centre of her should not be confused with having a life of your own
to which you should retreat,
she will drop you back down to the ground
alongside your hail-stricken heartbeat.
How is it you feel complete when your heart is debris
drowning on concrete?

Leaves fly from branches of trees like birds.
If she teaches you one thing
let it be to be free.
To have no restrictions on the speed at which you chase your needs,
even after lightning strikes you can still succeed,
caught up in the strongest gusts you can still
breathe.

Her aggression was not meant for you.
No one wants to be a disaster
no matter how natural.
It accumulated inside of her and she blew
spine-chilling surface winds into your eyes,
blindingly beautiful skies
disturbed by cries to go back in time.

Power flashes from lines. Light the way
for broken futures to collide.
She invites you along for the ride.
To make this more complex,
what nonsense,
a multiple vortex is more destructive than a single cyclone.
Don't let her drag you too far into the unknown
or rotate your thoughts until dust becomes your home.

If you're brave enough to cut off the air supply the vortex will weaken.

Roping out,
tornado choked with doubt
of her existence,
becoming a thin cut out
of her former self.

Trees creak as they straighten their backs to watch her dissipate.

You won't see the same her again.
Don't forget after the storm will come a rainbow.
A rainbow to frame
the lasting impression that became
all that remains
from the life-threatening game she played.

How colourful it is
is up to you.

16

My Morphine #2

Have you ever loved someone
who makes you enjoy dwelling in the rain?

Someone who, every time your phone screen lights up,
you want to see their name?

Someone who leaves you lost for words
when usually words are your forte?

Someone who you trust so bewilderingly
you want to get lost with them over and over again?

Someone who, to see that smile that makes you brace yourself,
you would gently brush away all of their pain?

Someone who makes you want to expand the capacity
and knowledge of your brain?

Someone who you know, deep down,
will never love you the same?

Unorthodox

Another day and it's already been said,
"How does it work when I get out of this bed?"
The antiquated taunt of how bad it's become
overshadowing the fight for a battle once won.

He knows me so well. "Do you fancy a brew?"
he asks, as he switches over to rhythm and blues.
A comfort like no other, how very English of me
to find solace in one mug. In one cup of tea.

The music washes over me,
my eyelids drop slightly,
swaying left to right,
I let out an almighty
CLICK of my fingers, my eyes are closed
quick! Snap back into the room before I believe my mind's trick.

He's dancing in, carrying a tune
alongside the beverage made to improve my mood.
Brewed to the colour his Mum had once said,
"The colour of that wardrobe, Son." It was engrained in his head.

The thanks were not lacking
they just wouldn't come out.
Even that comfort this time
couldn't fight the creeping doubt.

I listen but don't hear.
I look but don't see.

That's a lie, I hear fear,
that's a lie, I see debris,
left from all the times this has happened before,
I can't but if I could I would run for the door.

She'll say there's a reason for everything,
that it's all going to be grand,
but babe I'm an atheist,
I don't believe in God's plan.

I'm fading away,
soon my expression will be deadpan,
thrashing and kicking and scratching
like a madman.

It's not life-threatening,
you're okay,
it's going to pass.
Let's take some breaths,
name five colours,
how about a glass?

Of water this time because that tea just didn't suffice,
"Not offended I guess sweetheart but sort out your life."
It's a joke and I know it, recognition of words,
how exciting to feel something other than shaking and nerves.

Coming back down to earth
with a whack.
I'm tired
but that smile and "It's good to have you back."

It will get better.
Positivity is key.
Paramount importance for me to be free,
for me to be well again, for me to be me.

My Morphine #3

He makes me feel like I'm his when he speaks my name.
It could be the way I'm hearing it, he isn't to blame.
Let's face it, he probably does say every other person's name
with the same voice.

I forgive any of his actions
to keep on the receiving end of his reactions,
I replace other people's time for his interaction
because he's a profound distraction,
I try focusing on a positive outcome
to encourage The Law of Attraction
but it's infiltrated with negativity as I convince myself
I am not to his satisfaction.
I'm painfully conscious of my every move
and every stereotypical over-reaction.

Stay

New Year's Eve 2008,
my first kiss.
He took all words out of my mouth,
left me speechless.

Then spat them at me later.

Why didn't she just leave?

Have you ever tried to run up a downward moving escalator?

Like I said, it was New Year.
Everything was new,
nothing to compare this to,
on the borderline of *isn't he a bit old for you?*

But I'm of age
and he knows,
it was a game of numbers he was winning.
Spoiler Alert: this is how the rest of the game goes.

New Year is new beginnings
and all things good.
He told me he would protect me,
believable, he looked like he could.

A little bit of shelter
never hurt anyone
but a lot leaves you isolated
with nowhere left to run.

A predator's step number one.

I was taught to respect my elders,
of course I was going to respect him.
It's attractive when you meet someone
who, to see you all the time, will go out on a limb.

I had a kind heart.
The kind of heart that should be safe on earth
but when vulnerability is manipulated into weakness,
safety crumbles along with all self-worth.

He looked at me like he had all of the answers to my questions,
maybe because he was on Google at the time.
I put him in my locket, his face trapped against mine,
that should have been a sign written in bold, italics and underlined
       three times.

But in my naive teenage dreams
I was the lucky girl he liked.
So, I dropped my entire life.
And it shattered into pieces.

He was in my blind spot
and caught me off guard.
I collided with him unintentionally I thought
but he planned the wreck that left me permanently scarred.

He drove my life
like he'd just stolen it.
I couldn't figure out his algorithms
but he taught me so I would submit.

My fingerprints are imprinted with his.
If forensics dusted them down, they would find lines
mapping out all of the places he left his mark.
His eyes told me not to speak,
that I couldn't leave, that he was angry,
that it was my fault it had to get this dark.

The lies coated his tongue as seamlessly as saliva
and fell from his mouth as naturally as childhood teeth.
In front of others I was carried in the palm of his hand,
when they looked away he kept me under the soles of his feet.

And walked all over me.

He's a joke.
Not one I wanted to tell people.
The puppet-master tightened the strings
and the storyline became progressively evil.

Why did I let it happen?
Well, I lose patience with me too so I thought he had a point.
The only future I'd planned was with him,
he knew it was his to exploit.

I'd become a reflection of him.
Isn't it bad luck to break a mirror?
He took the most sacred thing
and how powerful he was became instantly clearer.

Sat in the toilet,
I had my blood on my hands.
That's exactly how it felt,
like I was responsible for tainting my body with his commands.

A mutated version of myself,
Frankenstein's monster.
A body inevitably stronger
but a mindset to match I was unable to conjure.

How do you scream for help
when you can't even breathe?
How could I speak out
when my voice made him seethe?

I listened to him
as though he never told me to shut up.
From a shelf full of bone china mugs
I was his paper cup.

He'd empty me,
throw me away like a convenient slut,
grind me into the ground
alongside every cigarette butt.

He told me
what I could or couldn't wear,
judged me
on whether I had or hadn't removed hair.

Turned wipers off in rain, lights off at night,
to remind me to be scared,
refused to take me home
if wanting to leave was something I shared.

I concealed my emotions
but he heard my internal screams.
He'd apologise insincerely for outbursts

with a smirk, like the cat who'd got the cream.

Why didn't I leave?

I forgot how to be in control,
what would I do if he wasn't?
He was the only comfort after violence,
somehow I found peace in his nonchalance.

I couldn't imagine a life without him,
maybe there wasn't one?
Every room, his. Every face, his.
Getting away wasn't an option.

I remember my Dad asked in an embrace,
"Don't you love me anymore?"
I hoped my agitation told him I was scared
because look what "love" had caused.

Then *he* wriggled into my comfort zone,
made me shudder and withdraw.

My eyelashes caught tears for me
whilst I detached from the rest of the world.
Physical contact with anyone
now left my toes curled.

I played the hand I was dealt, knowing if I bluffed
well enough I'd make it through another round,
numb to being beaten
time and time again into the ground.

When I tried to fold

he threatened to take his own life.
His blood on my hands as well as mine
when he's the one holding the knife.

I had to be on his good side,
that had become my state of play,
in case his threats spread further to anyone else
who might get in his way.

One day, I realised I had nothing left to risk.
Everything was lost.
So, as I felt like giving up,
I reached for the next hand that came along despite the potential cost.

I had a lightbulb moment.
Then it exploded over my head.
But I'd been to hell and back,
why wouldn't I run through glass to escape the burning dread?

I have to sleep in it, but he made my bed,
now I'm burning the sheets.
He tried to keep me prisoner, left me trapped inside my head,
yet he gets to be free?

It was an earthquake that shook my life
and I can't stop the aftershocks.
I trusted him and he betrayed me,
it's taken years for my trust to be unlocked.

It's like living with a sinkhole in the middle of your home.
You learn to live with it, around it, avoid it.
He plays the villain in every movie I watch
regardless of the atrocities they commit.

I've forgiven so much but it isn't my fault I can't forget.
In fact, it isn't my fault at all.
He's a joke and I'm going to tell him
over and over again until he gains no reaction anymore.

I'll say it on repeat
because his eyes told me not to speak.

My Morphine #4

Being good enough for yourself,
I like to think that can be taught.
Being good enough for someone else
is not a battle that should ever be fought.

But if he asked me to be his bag for life,
I would.
I'd hold his baggage and he'd use me over and over again
because love hurts this good.

Abscond

Where does it come from?
How does it start?
A traumatic event?
A broken heart?

What does it take to lose your mind?
To portray a smile containing nothing behind?

My poor brain.
My pathetic brain.
My useless brain,
I've just awoken and I'm already drained.

Or did I sleep?
I can't recall the night that just passed.
It doesn't switch off, my head
is a vast
vessel of worry, I'm trapped in my mind
but haven't I always been?
Only now, I can't find
any sense to be made within it.

Walking down the street,
"Cheer up girl, it might never happen!"
It already has, you moron,
but your humour is cracking!

I'm not going to walk down the road with a smile
plastered across my face,

you'd think I was mental.
I'm trying to hide that until I get out of this place.

"Big issue?"
"No, I've got plenty cheers."
Did I really just give that reply?
I could do with a beer.

That money could have gone to him.
I'm a terrible human being.
There is no method in my madness,
no reasoning for my fleeing.

They're talking about me in third person
as though I'm not sat in the same room.
I don't feel present, yet I'm wrapped in frustration.
I suppose I understand, I used to be naive to it too.

"Let's hang out next week!"
I'm sorry, no can do,
I've pencilled in a mental breakdown that day
that's going to hit me out of the blue!

It's never boring a life like this,
that's for sure.
The craziest I've ever been,
creating the sweetest art from the pure
honesty of my words,
if that's what you call it?
This passive aggressive poetry
or word vomit.

I've never made so much sense and so little

all at the same time.
I've never felt so tense yet so relaxed
in the complexity of my mind.

It feels uncomfortable,
like a cup of tea in a glass.
I'll have a coffee instead,
caffeine on which the doctor said I should pass.

I try not to think too far ahead,
two hours at a time, that seems fair.
But the future comes so fast upon us,
I'm lost, I'm confused and I'm scared.

It's like I'm a boat
sailing on choppy seas.
A bit of water splashes in and I cope,
any more than a splash gets the better of me.

When everything appears to be running like clockwork,
a little freak out to remind me I'm not okay.
But I believe creativity can accomplish more than common sense.
I'll hold on tight and I'll ride the wave.

I have one padlock
and I have one hundred keys.
Only one key will open the lock,
it's a matter of finding the one that pays heed.

I'm terrified to be okay
and to still not be good enough.
But I bet we're stronger than our excuses.
Let's place our bets and call its bluff.

My Morphine #5

I cheat myself out of my own time and energy.

I remember when it was 6pm
and sleeping was a future gift,
now it's 3am and I'm wondering who unwrapped it
and threw it into the pile of unwanted shit.

I've spent hours replaying our last encounter,
analysing every bit,
questioning whether life's getting me back
for the people I've hurt because I wasn't ready to commit.

I'm shuffling through my moonlit thoughts,
filing them in the appropriate places
but running out of room
for them all to fit.

This is so much more than logic
and nowhere near common sense.
I feel like the only thing that could help me sleep
is the comfort of his natural scent.

The Invisible Beast

It wraps its prodigious limbs around my chest,
pulls inwards, suffocating me.
Buries its extremities beneath my ribcage,
defeating the shield, restricting blood flow through my arteries.

The Invisible Beast
hangs dormant on my shoulders
awaiting one uneasy breath
to convince me I feel smothered.

Tears roll,
effortlessly.
Abuse at my own hands
mirroring the way he used to stifle me.

The numbness is a relief
otherwise this would hurt.
If it was attention I wanted there are easier ways
than this all-consuming threat brainwashing me to be an introvert.

I long to speak of other thoughts,
except positivity is swallowed by trepidation.
I long to tell you of the battle I just fought
but right now panic is my only obligation.

My Morphine #6

Fast forward to the weekend.
I'm hanging out with my... friend?

The soundtrack to our evening is Arctic Monkey's "Mardy Bum"
because he says I've got a face on.
I'm wishing it was "I Wanna Be Yours"
and he was serenading me with some kind of light-hearted allure.
I know the most appropriate tune would be "Snap Out of It"
because if someone doesn't grab my shoulders and shake, I am never
going to quit.

I might be putting one and one together and coming up with eleven
but I'll take it if the answer means we're side by side.
I'm not shy
but he's making me question whether these are emotions I should hide.

I Love You

I would set the scene but my body's defence mechanisms have
almost wiped that clean.

I couldn't tell you where we'd been,
only that I was sixteen
and what ensued was unforeseen,
at least to me, but he...

he was a well-oiled machine.

It's dark,
exhaust fumes burn the air,
the car is in park.
I'm unaware he's about to leave his first mark.

The warning lights weren't on,
how was I meant to know there was about to be a problem?
Let alone a big one.
To me, the fact a guy showed any interest was a phenomenon.

He didn't care about me,
how I took my tea,
that my least favourite soup was minestrone,
whether I enjoyed swimming in the sea
or about any information regarding my family tree.
He didn't care what I wanted to be,
whether I had aspirations and dreams
or even how my day at school had been.

He only cared what he could get for free
as he fumbled around with the buttons on his jeans.

It wasn't locked. I could have got out,
ran, or let out a shout
but I sat and barely entertained my doubt
because it was too early to cause a fallout.

It didn't matter if to my religion I was devout,
he knew it wasn't within my character to act out
and it wasn't something I was going to talk about.
Maybe.

Maybe why I didn't move was because
who would do anything that bad?
Outside the house containing my Mum and Dad.
Three older brothers with every reason to get mad.

If only my thoughts had clocked the ones he had
but to have attention from an older lad,
until this moment, had made me glad.
The one whose name I doodled in hearts in my yellow sketch pad.

Now, "You're not leaving until I'm finished," he said,
as he gripped his left hand around the back of my head
and forced it down to give him his.
I wanted to be magically in my bed.

Alone.

Maybe it was my actions he misread?
Or maybe I was a young girl who he misled?

Now the warning lights were burning my eyelids in blood red.
This was nothing like the romance stories, as a child, I'd been read.
It wouldn't have mattered how carefully I'd have tread,
he'd already planned this out in his head.

I should have bit it there and then,
taken one for the team for any future girls or women.
But my whole teenage body fell weak.
There was no room for me to speak.

Maybe words would have invited unwelcome critique,
already convinced I was some sort of freak,
the last thing I needed were comments on technique.
Or the opposite, some bullshit about how I was special or unique.

The silence I'd believed to be a part of his mystique
was masking a mentality petrifyingly bleak.
I convinced myself this is what women deserve and what all men seek,
as he thrusted bruises onto the insides of my cheeks.

"You're not leaving until I'm finished," he repeats.

I didn't care that I couldn't breathe.
By now passing out would have been a relief,
to put a halt on my childhood being taken by a thief,
to delay the onset of the inevitable grief.

The burning exhaust fumes imitate my burning desire
to be anywhere else but here.
I choke,
on my fear
as my mind kicks in to interfere
with thoughts of how I'll finish

this academic year
with a future that's about to become very unclear.

I swallow,
my shame.
The taste
of blame
drains the colour from my face.

No sign of an embrace,
only a hurried exit just in case
anyone caught *me* in all *my* disgrace.
Clutching the cross on my neck I hurried to the place
I called home.

Game face as I steadied my tone,
"Mum, Dad, I'm home. I'm going to bed."

Alone.

Days passed,
me wearing a mask,
constantly harassed with messages to keep quiet
but that part wasn't much of a task.

The more he kept a check
the tighter the noose got around my neck.
The more I realised what he did was wrong
my crippled personality struggled to belong,
thoughts of it repeating like an overplayed song.
To ask for help I knew I had to be strong.

I'm going to tell them.

I'm going to tell them because they'll understand.
They'll believe me when I say it was his command
and he emotionlessly forced my hand.
But what if they make me take a stand?

I'm going to tell them.
They'll know what to do, they always do.

They'll stop it before it escalates to something more taboo,
they will help me to start a new
and then they'll understand why,
the last time they went in for a hug, I involuntarily withdrew.

They'll believe what I'm telling them is true.

Mum will comfort me with her winter stew
whilst Dad does his best to undo this warped view
that all men will act this way too.
I'm going to.

"Mum... Dad...

I love you."

My Morphine #7

He makes me feel like,
without him, I would die
and when I'm with him
like I've never felt so alive.

How were we once strangers
when, before him, I can't remember my life
and thoughts of a future without him
make my depression take a nosedive?

Not Today

It's a normal day.
As normal as they get by now anyway.
Early morning,
Monday.

Said goodbye to Mum, she's got to get on her way,
work to be done.
College awaits me and my ten-thousand-word essay
which was definitely due last Thursday.

I scribbled the rest last night
watching *Pineapple Express* on Blu-ray
with the words, "Potential is nothing without persistence,"
in my teacher's voice, on replay.

Tea,
social media.
An encyclopaedia of selfies
filtered in sepia,
a blatantly subtle Facebook post
skirting around her recent heartbreak from Amelia.
Before I feel the urge to slide into her DM's to check it's not
too severe
I should probably get off of here.

Flick over to Asos,
they've got a sale on and maybe the jacket I saw is lowered in cost.
Out of stock
but I find a top

with the word "FAIL" printed across,
feels appropriate. Add to basket
along with those knee-high socks
which I am never going to wear, let's face it,
but they're the ones Becky's got
and with that mini-skirt she makes them look hot.

Realising an empty bank account can buy none of this,
I close the browser and find the willpower I'd dismissed.
Finally, I get to the shower.
I'll be ready to leave within an hour.

I emerge,
resist the urge to check Facebook again.
Hair's dripping wet, it was longer back then,
takes two minutes to dry these days, back then an easy ten.

Hair dryer, full heat, full power.
I'm living out of my shell before reverting back to wallflower,
singing acapella, murdering Rihanna's "Umbrella"
but in my head my performance is stellar.

"When the sun shines, we shine together!"
Hair flick!

Freeze.

Scream.

Silhouette darkens doorway,
he's come to take me.

How did he get in?

How do I get out?
He's blocking the only exit,
no one's going to hear me shout.

In my head I'm running,
in reality, hostage. Next move consequential.
Hair dryer mutates,
gun to temple.

Flashbacks assemble,
legs begin to tremble,
fall to knees,
beg him.

Second scream
accidental.

It's my brother.
Come to say goodbye.
I thought he'd left, now he's distressed,
so am I,
I'm a mess.
He holds me, we both cry.

Tears burst, cartoon-like,
from my eyes.
I sob for the future
that's gone awry.

"I'm a live wire," I say.

"I'm quite the electrician," he replies, "I'm used to a shock."

"One moment backtracking feels like scissors cut the rope and
I don't know when the fall will stop."

He says, "Who worries about scissors when you've got me?
Scissors can't beat rock."

He strums my vein. The one I've picked
to the chorus of "Jar of Hearts" replaying again and again,
vocal cords shredded from my inharmonic release of pain,
heartbeat amplified by the cranked-up strain.

Finger taps to stay present,
techniques to entertain
my distorted brain
from giving too much feedback that only leaves me drained.

"Are you going to be okay?"

I feel like I should ask him the same.

He leaves.
I take five more minutes to grieve,
return to my feet, legs still jelly,
breathe.

Talk myself out of finishing my hair
without having to speak.
I'll arrive at college,
hair wet, for the following week.

Isn't it funny how one trauma continues to traumatise
but not in a funny way?
"Potential is nothing without persistence,"
but not today.

My Morphine #8

I watch films I would never watch
and don't pay any attention,
then pray he doesn't lose the storyline
and ask me a question.

He'll clock the lead and exclaim, "She's fit!"
Although I probably agree,
I'm just wishing he'd said it
about me.

I try to persuade myself when he makes fun
it's the equivalent of pulling my hair in the playground,
when really, it's because we're mates, I'm one of the lads
and he thinks I'm "well sound."

I mean, he's open
and feels his feelings with me
but I guess that's because I'll share with anyone
given a mic, a stage and some company.

The Walk

Lift your chin.
Widen your stare.
Take it all in,
breathe in the fresh air.

I've never noticed it before,
the ever-changing woodgrain of the door.
My standard posture awkward and unsure,
head down, eyes at the floor.

The gate with its winding iron design.
Cracked paving stones no longer align.
The birds whistle in time.
To remind me I can't.

My gaze lifts towards the sky,
the Weeping Willow interrupts my eye,
its branches hanging lifeless and limp
to remind me to hold myself up high.

I follow the bark of the tree
to the floor,
allowing the earth to support me,
to show me what it's like to keep a strong core.

Appreciating the small things
through every pace. No one around
to exaggerate the smile on my face.
My shadow beside me, the sunshine leaves its trace.

What a place.

With the next step a twig snaps under my foot,
reminding me too much pressure can break any living thing.
A bush of holly stands in abundance to remind me there are many
    pricks in life,
don't mess with them and you won't feel the wounds they can bring.

Crisp, aged, brown leaves
under my soles,
reminding me it's crunch time
or I'll never achieve my goals.

The ditch filled with water from the night before
acting like a running stream,
fronts the barbed wire fence to the field beyond
to remind me some areas of life are off limits, or so it may seem.

The quagmire I've come across
reminds me of my college years with Mr Moss,
teaching my peers and I psychology,
thinking he was the boss.

If I'd listened more
this time in my life could be slightly less sore.

A car like the one I drive goes by,
makes me question if it's mine.
To remind me I'm an idiot.
But I remind myself of that all the time, so it's fine.

The friction of the tyres on the wet road

signals a *hiss* to my enemy.
My instinct tells me it's meant for him,
my mind tells me my only enemy is me.

The remnants of the exhaust fumes remind me I'll burn out
if my thoughts aren't restrained.
The void in the tarmac makes me acknowledge
I'm drained.

I take a left down Baccabox Lane.
Here comes the rain. Again.

Only, it feels even better than the sun.
It washes away the complexity for a moment,
for a moment I feel undone
of all the apprehension that's built up by the ton.

For a moment, I feel like someone.

My Morphine #9

How can he complete me
and I not complete him?
When I thought of love, I'd see red or pink,
now the colour of his eyes seeps in.

He is the flame
and I am the wax,
the brighter he burns,
the more I melt against the glass.

If we can sing like losers
at the top of our lungs on the first car ride,
how is this not already a work of art
and a one-off find?

I've never been into astrology
but I'm reading both our star signs,
only believing them when they sound like our stars
are perfectly aligned.

Routine

Hands and knees
head heavy
can't catch breath
muscles shake
eyes wide
eyes blind
ears deaf
rolling
writhing
thoughts compressed
knuckles white
teeth crunch
fear manifests
room distorts
violent predator
hostage held perplexed
car crash
airbag failed
full impact to chest.

How much time straining to expel tears do I have to invest?

Can't.
Continue.
Help.
Don't help.
Help.
I don't want help.
Help.

I don't need help.
Please help,
I'm dying,
"Someone help me!"

I don't recognise the sound,
it's surely my voice?
I don't recognise my actions,
they're surely my choice?

Minutes ago I was smiling, perhaps even a laugh,
what changed
to make it look like I'm trying to choreograph
an expressive one man play?

I've been here before,
shredded vocal cords,
hands clawed,
yet it isn't familiar this stone-cold floor.

I've been here before,
yet I still can't retain
that this will pass
or what triggers me to stray.

Tears are not rolling but streaming
through the grey of the storm clouds surrounding me, getting in
        my way.
This happens day to day, for what is it I'm making me pay?
Why did I betray myself after all my hard work?

I've been here before,
yet I still can't retain

that this will pass
or what triggers me to stray.

Physical pain from mental foul play.

How many times do I need to mislay my sanity?
How many times does this have to replay
before I learn to outweigh the negativity?
To slay the demons?

My momentum has wavered.
The force needed to go forwards again
is not something I savoured
from the last.

Expectedly unexpected,
bewildered, disconnected,
sweating, frozen,
eyes powerlessly closing.

I'm not sure I can,
peel my empty shell off the floor to try once more.

Until tomorrow.

My Morphine #10

When the pain hits
it's like The Borrowers have snuck into my chest,
they're pulling at different sides of my heart
causing distress,
screaming different instructions from within of what I
should do,
"He's not worth it!"
"You're gonna get hurt!"
"He probably feels the same as you!"

Am I in love?

Or am I in love with the idea of being in love with him?
When really, I want to rip off his clothes with lust
but I don't want to be labelled as a slut
so I'm using love as a pseudonym.

Brother

Standing at six foot and one inch tall.
Stood as sturdy as a brick wall.
A wall you can't believe would ever fall.

But it did begin to crumble,
first in small pieces and then all at once.
We accompanied every trip and we felt every stumble.

Apparently I got him through.
Why can't I get me through?
I'd have treated him differently if I knew.

I'm sorry I didn't understand his desperation.
I'm sorry I couldn't appreciate his frustration.
I'm sorry I didn't respect his uncontrollable vexation.

I prayed, yet I didn't believe in a God.
Asking for God's help I felt like a fraud,
my coping mechanisms were undeniably flawed.

He says, "I couldn't have done it without you."
Only now do I feel I could truly help,
now I have an insider's view

I scream, "I don't want to do this anymore!"

He says, "But honey, don't you remember what you told me before?

You are destined to win this war...

because you are the only one in it."

That's how I know I can do it.

When he rebuilt that wall,

he rebuilt it higher and stronger than ever before.

My Morphine #11

I look at him.
He's already looking at me.
He looks away.
I try, but my eyes fixate.

The background noise whittles down to only the beating
of my heart,
I can feel it beating in time to his even if he can't.
The Borrowers are shrieking that giving it back to the rightful
tenant and evicting him is smart
but how can a connection between two only be felt on
one part?

The only thing in focus is him.
And questions of, "Was it a coincidence or did he mean
to look too?"
"Can he sense that my eyes haven't yet moved?"

Everything is still.

Mind Games

One day, when my mind starts to clear,
I'll be like a firework in the rain.
One that goes up and explodes into a dazzling sea of colour,
never to fall back down again.

Despite the storm and the dampening mist,
my light will glow, my warmth will insist
that I have conquered the journey from rock bottom to sky.
Those who've watched will smile and release their sigh.

The chemical reaction will be finally right,
the sky will illuminate into day before descending back into night.
The resonance in my outburst will signal that you can do it too.
Be patient in your preparation then be brave and light your fuse.

My Morphine #12

His eyes drew in my heart
in pencil.

Rather than seeing it as temporary,
I thought I saw potential.

My Biggest Fear

It's gained momentum not by the day but by the second.

I've felt it build as I've watched each *tick*
of my bedroom clock,
whilst each *tock* builds agitation,
contributing to the inflammation of discontent.

It's going to be too late.
I can't communicate because of my mental state
and I'm scared
that it's going to be too late one day.

One day I'll awake and there will be no undoing my mistake
because you are gone.
That which I'd fought for all along, to be nice to you,
will no longer be an option.

The only option is to be sorry.
So, so sorry.
And wallow away the rest of my days, playing through alternative
ways in my already dishevelled brain. What does that gain?

Hate is a strong word but the actions,
so easy.
It's not you it's me,
I don't blame you for not believing a line so cheesy.

I don't blame you. I don't know why I'm acting like I do
and I'm sorry.

So, so sorry because you didn't raise me this way,
you raised me to exude love no matter how heavy my demons weigh.

I've never lied to you before,
yet you still question, "Are you sure?"
when I tell you I'm okay.
I've never lied to you before.

Until now.

I'm lost.
I'm lost like our home movies on old VHS,
I need to be converted to work in this modern world
before you can gain access.

I'm a closed book of poems you want to read.
My brain goes as deep as a submarine,
the deeper I go, the less light
can penetrate the waters to reach me.

I'm always vacant
because the lock on my abandoned memories is broken.
Your reactions are heightened,
I'm learning to neglect emotion.

I'm racing the go-kart you bought us as kids,
headfirst into the wall I've built,
cutting through the rope of the tyre swing you made
with my razor-sharp tongue,
un-tying one end of the zip line
to make it more difficult for us to reach the other side,
hammering, with my heavy heart, on the slats
of the tree house you built when we were young.

Oxygen is rapidly rusting the swing set
because I'm not inhaling my share,
I hear the hum of lullabies used to sing me to sleep
but the words are no longer there.

I'm making a molehill
out of the mountain you once were.
I got your eyes
but trying to see through them is one big blur.
I maintain that what you don't know can't hurt you
but I know you create scenarios in your head and it's worse.

You have a mouth full of questions,
my answers are lodged in my throat.
I can't stand that everything I do affects you, so I sit
whilst reflecting on the chance of curing my fear being so remote.

I don't want to be interesting or funny,
that warrants attention.
"Too close for comfort" has never rang so true,
I'm looking for a cure because I left it too late for prevention.

"Leave me alone!"
I don't know if I'm talking to you
or my own prying mind.

"Please. Stop speaking."
Again, you?
Or my internal shrieking?

"Please don't touch my crawling skin."
I'll peel back every thin layer
tainted with tactlessness and sin.

I'm sorry I wiped away your touch.
I know your intention I misjudged
but I've spent a decade wiping away his and this reaction won't budge.
Soft kisses sit on my skin like paper cuts.

How can I feel like you're trying to reduce my rights
when you're trying to reduce my pain?
How can I feel like you're holding me back
when you're holding back the knife from my vein?

You're gathering me back together,
I'm giving you one more wrinkle every time my silence increases
    the strain
and I'm sorry.
You didn't get to say goodbye to her.
But she feels so much peace.
She couldn't take on the world as it is now,
she said it's a job for me.
I agree
but an initiation period is routine with any newly filled vacancy.

If my job had been as unrewarding as yours has been recently
I'd have quit but you work harder.
Every time I hoist up the anchor,
you throw it back down with a reminder that it's safer in the harbour.

You've never had an empty nest
and you know you never will,
so you reinforce it with the toughest materials
and glue it together with the strongest silk.

Your love has been known to move monsters for me,
mine moves you to tears.

On the outside you're the sturdy frame around our family photos,
inside you're on your knees praying for my nightmares to disappear.

The vent of my heater warps like it's going to eat me
because I've stared at it too long.
You text me even though you're only four rooms away,
I'll wish I'd heard your voice more when it's no longer an option.

I'm sorry I can't feel for you. My frozen heart
pumps cold blood around my body and it's making me numb.
I should treat you better knowing you're the ones who never falter,
knowing you're there at the end of any episode regardless of
      the outcome.

I'm a constant contradiction of, "Help me!"
"No, don't."
I still hang on your every word
but sometimes I like to cut the rope.

You're there every time
at the bottom to catch me if I can't stop,
your love travels faster than my thoughts
and you anticipated this before I dropped.

I don't like goodbyes since the thought became permanent
but you need one before I leave,
I want to slow down and take in this moment
but my brain has the body of an athlete.

You wind me up like a Jack-in-the-box
but it's a toy you've never seen before,
you aren't to know you're cranking up the tension,
whether you'll be met with a children's party clown or the lunatic
from *Saw*.

The small things that make me scowl now
are the things I know I'd miss the most.
The sounds that make me twitch
will be the sounds I'll wish were still this close.

I wish I could let you love me in the way you want to,
I've never seen something so unconditional.
You've changed your views on everything for me,
to be more modern and less traditional.

"One hour at a time," you'll say
and I know you understand.
"You might die tomorrow, just go for it!"
I can take that kind of command.

We've all felt the heat
on this last trip around the sun,
something has to give
to relieve some pressure on the next one.

My biggest fear is that one day it will be too late
and I won't have fixed it before you're done
but thank you for letting me learn to walk again
before I learn to run.

So, this is me, opening up my closed book of poetry for you to read.
In the hope it goes some way to setting us free.
To overcoming my biggest fear
and not sitting on the stairs for conversations so there's a barrier in
between.

Just wait.
I will always come back to you.

Just wait,
if you have time.

You see, you wrote that poem.
And I realised,
you're the reason that I write.
You are the reason I am alive.

My Morphine #13

My girlfriends will say it's his loss
but I know it's mine
because if he could see what he's doing
to my heart and my mind,
he wouldn't think it was fine,
he would think he'd crossed a line,
he'd say, "I'm sorry, I should have read the signs."

The emotion comes in waves
and like a wave to the shore,
he washed over me, unconsciously,
shifting pieces of me to suit him until I didn't recognise me anymore.

I Win

That's just it, you do, you bother me.
Getting in the way of any chance of harmony
I could have hoped to have within my life,
now all I have are my troubles and my strife.

Stemming from you, yes
you with the hair,
with the teeth, with those eyes,
with the same chavvy clothes you still wear.

At least that's what I imagine when I see you
through my mind's eye every day.
Eleven years may have passed
but how you look and what you'd say
remain as clear as a bell,
ringing continuously in my ear.
Your silhouette in my dreams
makes me convinced you're still here.

Who'd have thought four months of an expected eighty years
could have such an impact? Could leave such lasting fear.

In that moment,
when innocence was lost,
I knew it would never be the same,
I felt a layer of frost
freeze over my heart
as a weakness struck my knees.

Game face girl, game face,
you've got people to please.

You're etched in my memory.
I guess that's the way it will always be?
I'll store you in the bitter part,
the part with no access to my heart.

I've come a long way
since that fateful day
when you grabbed my arms, my legs,
closed the door, drove away.

"Say goodbye to your house, you'll never see it again."
Don't make me laugh darling, you underestimated my zen.

An exterior of calm I obtained as you drove like a psycho.
Ironic, a word you once used to insult my big bro
and oh, by the way, my Dad is not an alcoholic,
you really spewed some shit. Disconnected and robotic.

He's a man.
A real man.
He's how you treat a girl. You could learn a thing or fifty
if you weren't shut off from the real world.

You took away any feeling.
And the rest,
my conscience, my pride, my trust,
me at my best.

But I can get that back my dear.
You can't ever change your eyes,

embedded with evil,
riddled with lies.

Poor you.

You're stuck with you.
I don't have to be,
not anymore,
I'm ready to be free.

I forgive you.

Not for you, for me.
But I do, I do because you see,
I'm glad it was me.
Me you deceived, not another lady.

Without what you did
I wouldn't be this smart.
So thanks, you bastard,
for helping me create this piece of art.

My Morphine #14

My heart is sweating
from all its hard work,
The Borrowers are singing under the shower
to R.E.M "Everybody Hurts."

I want to cry
but then he'll ask why
and I'll have to lie
and say, "I'm hormonal, it's just that time."

Then he'll comfort me
with his skin on mine
and I'll lose more control
than when I caught his eye.

Insignificant

Spit-shined shoes, high-tops,
slingbacks, trainers,
socks under sandals,
unnecessary layers?

Infant size six
that Velcro fasten,
brown, leather, heeled boots,
less for comfort, more for fashion.

The flip flop of flip-flops,
designer labels from knockoff shops,
cream and navy, two-tone Brogues,
petite slippers wishing they were still at home.

A saunter, a stroll,
a fast walk, a shuffle.
Time taken, pick up the pace,
time's a tickin', time to hustle.

No interest in the commotion
or the rest of the scene,
crouched close to foetal for comfort,
each story unfolding below the knee.

As I await my company,
they're oblivious to inconspicuous me,
in the place that can take you anywhere,
I wonder where their footprints shall lead.

Headphones in,
no theme tune playing,
me and my one bag,
not lonely, only liberating.

Excitement in a bundle,
nerves just a tad,
no thoughts of where I've been,
only adventures to be had.

My heartbeat is tame,
no effort to be made,
I'm ready to feel insignificant,
for my worries to become the same.

I wrap up my poem,
slip my pen where it's held.
I could get used to this feeling.
I glance to the screen.

Flight FR9163   CANCELLED

My Morphine #15

How do I feel safe with him
when I've given him the ability to hurt me more than anything?

Discovering him was like discovering a whole new language,
an unspoken one,
not one I could teach to anyone else,
not even him. Not even after this long.

He is the sun
and I am a shadow,
which is to say,
to him, I unintentionally belong.

One Night Stand

Boom, boom, boom.
My heart.
Echoing your *knock, knock, knock.*
My eyes dart at the clock.

You're late.
I make you wait.
For all of fifteen seconds
as I straighten up my hair that's already straight.

I push down the handle
along with my eagerness.
A *creak*, mimicking my self-questioning,
adrenaline rushes to my blushing cheeks.

Eyes of intent greet me.
Your air of arrogance enters before you,
passing my self-control making its swift exit,
this is no Brexit.

"Drink?"
"After the day I've had? Absolutely!"
I haven't had that kind of day
but you don't need to know that, this small talk is only in the way.

If dignity came served in a tumbler, over ice, with a slice
and tasted like, "Kraken?"
"You brought Rum? Sweet!"
then I would drink it neat.

But my dignity slips away
as seamlessly as the liquor wonders astray
into my bloodstream.
You're ready to play.

I noticed you scan my body
with those plunge pool eyes,
they're black right?
Funny, so are mine.

I spent just enough time making myself look fine,
just enough effort to look hot plus a little extra effort
to make it look like I haven't had to make the effort
to look this hot.

Your weakness was emphasised
when your plunge pool eyes stopped at my thighs.
The upper handed to me, I'm in control
but you intended me to be,
didn't you?

You're unaware of my reasoning but for that I thank you.

It might be the Kraken telling me to krack on
but I'm all ears,
inhibitions disappear,
our chemistry shifting up a gear.

As our movements intensify
our bodies become further intertwined,
my effervescence screaming availability,
the perfect cover for my harboured hostility.

Your focus is pinpointed
on my agility,
my not-so-graceful motion
and my gnarly flexibility.

I was hooked when you lifted me
off of my feet.
Those thighs, remember? They gripped you.
We both felt the heat.

Since that moment I was planning my retreat.

I parallel my libidinous temperament with yours,
overflowing temptation encouraging me to explore,
pressure passes from my body to yours,
I privately question how much longer I can endure.

I can feel the intoxication
but I can't gauge the cause.
It could be you, the rum
or the fear of unloosing my most substantial flaw.

All is not as it appears
but you're tantalising my every sense
even through swallowed tears
so I persevere.

Because I am worthy of this liberation,
your generosity and stimulation,
but my mind is rejecting your invitation
and I'm writhing away into my foreseen damnation.

I feel as though I'm choking on my extreme palpitations,
the adrenaline that flushed my cheeks has now activated a fight
        or flight flirtation,
as I attempt to convince my mind that this is not an obligation,
you're reading my body language and sense my hesitation.

We both retract.

That trigger word, "Relax."
I shake and I shake off my unwelcome flashback,
a colossal drawback
of being damaged goods.

To feel like your body has been hijacked.

This is shaping up to be one spectacular
anti-climax.

My Morphine #16

I sing those car ride songs in the shower
like a fool
and rehearse our conversations to the door frame
because it has a bit more substance than a flat wall.

How can an elbow or fingernail be perfect?
Or a person be the perfect amount of tall?
Although the way he dresses isn't to everybody's taste,
I think his fashion no-sense is pretty cool.

Me pretending to act naturally
has got me looking like a real oxymoron,
so has trying to articulate something that can only be felt
but I can't stop going on.

I worry when we're not talking
in case he's talking to someone else, for one.
For two, I need to know he's safe,
I can't bear the thought of him suddenly being gone.

I'm getting ahead of myself.

I'm putting all my eggs in his basket
so when he takes it to the checkout my heart can be spent.
Then I'm asking for a refund even though I'm not the one with
the receipt
and the purchase was made with my consent.

Perspective

I blamed you
for everything that you would do,
you would do to screw
me over to a point I didn't know who I was anymore.

I spent countless hours contemplating how to settle the score.
You're the reason I withdrew!
You made me endlessly deliberate ways to redo
this life you'd created for me to debut.

Only, today I saw you from a different point of view.
In that moment I knew.
How am I blaming something so undeniably beautiful?
Something that allows me to explore every avenue.

My respect for you grew
as rapidly as I was falling.

I'd been waiting for too long in a queue
of countless people who blamed you too,
waiting for my turn
to take something back for all of the times you'd left me to burn.

Today it appeared someone had adjusted the hue.
You weren't black and white anymore,
you were bursting with colour.
Not just raging red or chilling blue.

Today I realised you're breaking me through.

Today I realised you're letting me renew.

One day maybe I'll reflect
the beauty you were able to gracefully project
up at me today, onto someone else who has lost their way,
who is blaming you. Maybe I'll help them to see what is true.

I don't blame you anymore.
You're amongst the things which I simply adore.

I thank you for this day.
I thank you for showing me the way
and not asking me to repay you in some way.
You are my world. You've given me reason to stay.

Perspective.
Change your perspective.

My Morphine #17

I dared to dream of something
I would never wake up to
but love doesn't know boundaries of waiting
until it's reciprocated, it just seizes you.

Why would he want me if when he looks at me,
he sees himself?
He is all I believe I am now
and he already loves him, he doesn't need me to show him how.

He's going to break me
into tiny pieces of a puzzle.
I'll rebuild with the outer edges,
working my way to the centre, hoping it becomes clearer despite
the struggle.

If You Knew

Dear Jem,
I won't ask how you're doing,
I've been there, I know.
I'm writing to reassure you your story is worth pursuing
despite his abysmal cameo.

Saving yourself for "the one" was important to do.
Thoughts of living in the wrong order intimidated you.
Marriage inevitable,
sex outside of it, not an avenue
you'd dare take.
Anything reinforced to us as children we ingurgitate like cake.

Now you're left to retch on this slice of tart,
too gut-wrenching to swallow.
Too unyielding to digest
because it doesn't reach the expectations you strove to follow.

You craved his attention.
But not that kind.
The anaesthesia of manipulation
numbing your mind,
lights on and someone home
but dimmed so the control was hard to find.
An exit with a code to crack left you confined.

When reality becomes something you've only encountered
        in fiction,
how do you cope?

It's like hitting black ice, knowing you can't stop the slide,
with nothing to hold on to but hope.

Things like this don't happen to people like you
so this can't be your slippery slope.
Except they do. And it did,
so let's try and navigate this crossroad.

Your naivety being a weakness
even though you were a child,
the questioning his affection because, afterwards,
he smiled.

You're not going to hell.
You're going through it right now.
Yes, you said "no" and no,
you didn't ask for it before you opened your mouth.

No should have been enough first time,
let alone second or third,
and regardless of no your silence should have been heard.
It's not your fault that silence he preferred.

When you tried to relax
so the pain would be deterred,
that was not you trusting his every word,
that was brave.

It did not mean you'd caved
because you wanted to get out unscathed
and if he's done the same to someone else
you aren't responsible for how he behaves

just because you tried to love someone
who needs more than what love can do.

Just because you saw him as human
despite his inhumane view.
Don't condemn yourself for being gullible
when he spoke fluent blackmail like truth.

You'd say, "Don't mistake my kindness for weakness,"
knowing full well it was no mistake.
But kindness is never an invitation to abuse what you can take,
to constrict until they break,
to coerce into a bed they didn't make.

Don't let the scent of humiliation keep you awake.
Rip off the sheets,
burn the pillows, those can be replaced.
Use a night light to prevent harmless objects shifting in shape.

Captivity is familiar,
making decisions, a treat.
Don't stand at the window wondering,
go and stand barefoot in the grass and feel freedom at your feet.

Making decisions for yourself when you've been conditioned
to believe you're always wrong is no mean feat
but you don't need to know where you're going
to sit in the driver's seat.

Like a poet on stage reminiscing their battle
when it's clear they're still wielding their sword and shield,
you're wearing an armour, pretending it's nothing you can't handle,
petrified your fate is sealed.

Forgiveness is a minefield.
You can't reclaim what he stole
but that doesn't mean what's left is dishonourable.
Or that you need to repent and cleanse your soul,
or abuse can be excused if it's tolerable,
or your life needs to acquire quality control
because your watercolour painting has been smothered in charcoal.

I believe you.
And I am the only opinion that counts.

You won't just "get over it" like ignorance will announce,
so don't entertain it with "yeah, I know" and a deep burial of doubt.
You may feel worthless,
that doesn't mean your love can now be bought at a discount.

You'll confide in the wrong people
but it won't cause damage,
turns out public speaking
will help you manage.

The air may be as thick as him right now
but you'll continue breathing despite the challenge
and if sex is ever a term and condition again,
Jem, honey, you don't want the package.

Custard Creams no longer mean you hear his voice,
you prefer a Bourbon but it's nice to know you have the choice.
One day you'll befriend someone who shares his name
and you'll know that's the only thing they share the same.

Don't wither trying to be a delicate flower
waiting to bloom,

future-you is a cactus, be prickly
if you need some room.

Take the faith you used to put in others and bathe in it
until it seeps through your pores,
let it wash away his fingerprints.
Then watch as it opens doors.

You can't force clouds to disperse
but the sun is there even when you can't see it,
it will stay strong until it breaks through
and ensure your darkest nights are moonlit.

Fear comes before bravery.
You have a future and it's here with me.
At last he is an afterthought. That is, after you.
That is how it should be.

You see, a leopard can't change its spots
but appearance does vary depending on climate.
Don't surrender to your current conditions or overanalyse
your predisposition, change is constant.

Oh, and let them comfort you
before comfort agitates.
Sealed with a loving
handshake.

Jemima.

My Morphine #18

I want to learn about him every day
and be allowed to explore
but I gave so much of me straight away
he doesn't need to know more.

I don't know my heart anymore,
I only know ours.
Although we've only been in the same room for the last
twenty minutes,
all these thoughts racing around have made it seem like hours.

My butterflies begin to morph
back into caterpillars.
Maybe the unavoidable heartbreak will be worth it
when I feel more love looking in the mirror?

The Borrowers are digging a grave in my heart
to bury the idea of "us" before I have the chance to become bitter.

Dear Brain

You almost made me leave.
Caused friends and family to grieve
the loss of someone who was still there, caught beneath
a lack of belief in herself.

But for now I think it's safe to say that neither of us are moving out,
so let's try to understand what each other are about,
shall we?

Mind and I have been figuring out our differences for a while.
Mind believes she can bring you around to our way of thinking.
Look, we understand that you prefer to freestyle
but it doesn't work for us when you leave us immobile.

We'd appreciate a reconcile
so we can work together on this new lifestyle,
towards which you've become very hostile.
Together, we could compile something worthwhile.

When you aren't so busy keeping a low profile,
you've shown you can be pretty versatile,
good company,
sometimes you even let me crack a smile
but then you run a mile.
Why do you do that?
Two steps forward and one step back.

Excuse me while I break it down.
Sorry, I mean while I have a breakdown.

Banging my head against a brick wall used to be an expression,
these days it's a mechanism to cope
with the aggression,
the obsession,
the depression
that sure is manic,
volcanic,
at times satanic.
The hellish look in my eyes when it's time to panic
as my subconscious and conscious scramble to establish a more
    attuned dynamic.

An emotional pain so intense
I use physical pain in self-defence.

You see, anxiety and depression are my friends.
The kind who are always there for you
but like to embarrass you in public too.

I've learnt, when they come knocking,
let them in.
Make a brew, sit with them,
that's how I win.

I've tried to push them away before
but they taught me I can't live without them
through lessons that used force.
So now I let them stay.
Allow emotion to spill out in any way that feels natural that day,
cry, scream, wail, shake, an expressive one-man play.

To fit in any positive feelings

first I have to make room,
expel the negative however I see fit
then when I'm ready, I'll resume.
Weaker in the moment, sure,
but afterwards, money can't buy the strength you exude.

Money also can't buy happiness, that's what they say,
but what's absolutely terrifying is when nothing can.
Not even the love of my family,
that's when I question my decision to stay.

It was the most surreal thing,
finally wanting to live again and realising I no longer knew how to.
This world is so different to the last one I knew,
like someone Photoshopped me in but forgot to airbrush me smooth.

I awoke to two new family members I didn't know were due,
allowance to swear in front of my parents
because the sound of my voice was a breakthrough.
I used to be a chameleon. Now I'm the elephant in the room.

Growing up my lucky number was two,
since mum said, "With two you're never lonely," and I believed it to
        be true.
Until I realised you can be lonely with twenty-two,
two hundred and twenty-two,
twenty-two million, two hundred and twenty-two thousand, two
        hundred and twenty-two.
You can be sat in a room with many multiples of two
and still feel like you have only you.

My body is a prison
with a chief that won't listen.

Inmate for life, no chance of parole
or escape plans to come to fruition.

People look at me like they can catch it.
Maybe they can?
I'd argue, more likely, they don't understand.
If only they understood that they don't understand,
that would lend more of a helping hand
than wrapping me in bubble wrap and sending me in padded
    packaging
to a secure room where I can be manned.

Their corner-eye glimpses of inquisitiveness don't falter,
unaware that their customary expressions have altered.
All I can envisage is the spider in my bath
and how he didn't deserve to be greeted with my wrath.
I imagine how he felt towards my judgemental scream,
I imagine as I question if I broke his self-esteem.

I'm not mental.
They're judgemental.
I'm not mentally ill,
I'm mentally intriguing.

There's something very beautiful about being mentally intriguing.
I'm not talking about how sometimes I forget how to breathe in
without counting, I mean the ability to tap in
to another dimension that some people will only ever dream in.

Stability is comfortable
but also restricting.
Soundness of mind is reassuring
but also limiting.

Plus, when I'm mentally intriguing
I know how to behave.
Trying to act "normal" feels like someone turned up gravity
and it's sucking me through the floor into an early grave.

Maybe I see the world through fanatical eyes?
Or maybe some only open theirs up to desirable skies?
My head is in the clouds, not because I'm high,
because they hang low and climates don't compromise.

When I'm left cold and without light
though the sun remembered to rise,
I'm reminded if I don't meet expectations
I am not obliged to apologise.
Like that time I felt nothing
plummeting from a fourteen-thousand-foot skydive
because happiness isn't real and neither is fear,
they're in your mind.

The mind being the most powerful tool you own
which is why the enemy fights you there because that's where it gets
you alone.

Head or heart?
Is never a question. My head wears the trousers
which explains why I feel upside down and the wrong way around
during any romantic encounters.

How can I feel everything
and nothing within one breath?
How can I feel empty
yet simultaneously as heavy as my Dad's eyelids after a bottle of red?
How can I want to live

and the next minute be planning my death?

Forget monsters underneath,
mine spoon me in my bed,
body's exhausted ready to sleep
but the memo didn't make it to my head.

Maybe the problem is it's midday
and I'm forcing myself to sleep,
not because I'm tired, so something may have changed
when I awake to pull me out of this whimpering heap,
that seemingly there is no reason for me to be in.

My body
feels stronger than it should ever have had to be.
Yet still, I'll speak to you with the honesty of a child
if with the delicacy of one is how you treat me.

If I was screaming because I'd trapped my finger in a door
it would be easy to feel sympathy,
trapped inside my own head
the instinct is to criticise and flee.

But please,
try to imagine feeling so anxious
that the sound of someone parting their lips
makes you feel you could rip your eardrums out with ease,
or the texture of loved one's words makes you bite
because they torment your teeth,
or your clothes touching you the wrong way
will leave you twitching for weeks.

I'm not mad at you. I'm mad at my irrational response

and allowing my life to become this bleak.
Someone else's inspiration to live
when I'm still on a 4:3 ratio myself each week.

"Suicide is selfish" is not an opinion,
it's wrong.
What's selfish is expecting someone to live for you
when their pain is excruciating and they feel they can't belong.

If I hear someone say "there's no need to cry"
I lose my shit.
If there was no need to cry,
why would our bodies insist we do it?

When I can't let people touch me,
the familiar tears stroke my cheeks and tell me it's okay.
It can be difficult to differentiate between a breakdown
and any other bad day.

Sometimes I get excited and my body panics
because it takes these foreign feelings the wrong way.
When I consider being more to someone than a passing thought,
I know I can't commit to that, so I pull away.

Beautiful minds with the ability to travel anywhere. Without moving.
Why does mine travel to a gloomy place?
When I don't hesitate on a bridge,
I've won a race.
For life.

Suppressed feelings caused too much trauma,
now I don't attempt to game face.
When oxygen I need to survive suffocates me,

I feel like I belong in outer space.

I am rough around the edges
and straight through the middle,
my language is encrypted
and my actions contort as riddles.

Autopilot is not an option when your memory is fickle.
When it's bad, I forget how good it gets.
When it's good, I forget how bad it gets.
I'm wary of good because how bad the ensuing crash will be
leaves me in suspense.

It's like I developed a sixth,
seventh, eighth sense
for things
that don't need to be sensed.

If I focus on one thing for too long, I'll fall,
so I count as I'm walking down steps.
My large intestine is a spitting cobra releasing venom
leaving me temporarily blind to the present tense.

Every movement takes more energy than it should.
I can walk as instinctively backward as I can forward.
Headphones in, no music,
muffles the external tortures.

My skin is worn out,
like me.
Baths became an overused comfort,
like tea.

I never drink decaf and I do that for me
because despite what doctors have me believe,
no one was ever diagnosed with something off the back
of lack of decaf coffee.

Don't let me fool you into a false sense of security,
I think too much to be logical.
"But writing makes you feel happy?"
No, writing makes me feel. Full stop.

I load my pen with pain and I spiel,
because this is what happens when mental intrigue reaches
        fever pitch,
we create something that makes the pain appeal.
And there's something to be said for a rhyme
to help people believe something is real.

The day I began to lose my mind
I began to find myself.

That is, when I realised
it's okay to ask for help.
Even if it means waking someone up.
Self-sabotage is enticing but it's a relief when someone interrupts.

You see, two steps forward and one step back is not a royal fuck up,
it's still one step forward.
So I take the bad with the good,
and embrace the disordered and awkward.

Now, I look forward to tasting that first tea (of many) in the morning
because it means I've made it through another night.
Progress is progress,
regardless of how slight.

My Morphine #19

It takes a while to heal
when you put your heart on the line
and someone crosses it.

I'm grateful he's pushed me
to be much more than I already was
and on many occasions been the reason I didn't quit.

Now, I want to be what he is to me
to someone else.
But that is a lot to ask.

He was never mine.
It's time for me to reluctantly
take a step back.

I

I could have been

I would have been

I should have been

I long to be

I want to be

I desire to be

I wish I was

I pray I was

I feel at a loss.

I aim to be

I will be

I insist to be

I have decided to be

I intend to be

I endeavour to be

I know I can

I know I can

I can create my "I am."

My Morphine #20

And still,
I'm looking at him.

He looks at me.

I look away.

The Friend in the Green T-Shirt

This is a love poem!
Not in the way you may think,
the way many already do
or the way I once did.

But it is a love poem.
This is love at its most sublime,
this is love if it fell in love,
this is love being able to tell the time.

He caught me off guard
like those toilets with a sensor flush,
you sit back too far
and it turns into a bidet mid push.

He looked at me like there are pages in between,
not just a cover.
He intimidated me, in a motivational way,
made me want to write more so there is more to discover.

He made me feel inadequate.
It was unintentional but he did
because there is nothing common about his sense,
his mind is unconventional.

His words are gold dust.
Words I treasure knowing they exude quality,
they cover my days but don't weigh me down,
a layer of protection when I can't tame my curiosity.

It's dangerous. Being close to someone
when you are prone to obsessive behaviours.
When you meet someone
and immediately believe they are your saviour.

I know at times my passion far outweighed his, which hurt,
but the reality is it's done me countless favours.

He looked at me
like an abstract painting.
Reading into me,
not troubled that figuring me out involved watching and waiting.

He fitted a window and a door in the wall I'd made,
handed me the key without expectation, this was no trade.
Light seeped through the window where we spoke of
        personal crusades
until I was ready to concede and remove the barricade.

When others stepped back
as though they could catch my condition,
he stepped up.
Looking at me as though catching me had been his lifelong ambition.

And he did.
He caught me with strength
which far outweighed his stature.

He taught me we ride waves on surfboards not rubber dinghies,
that is much harder to master.
You create unnecessary work if you don't equip yourself with the tools
to make sure you're looked after.

He reminded me some cuts are deep enough to require stitches,
not covering with a plaster.
He showed me laughter can take back control if you're brave enough
to do it in the face of disaster.

When our friendship narrowed to a one-way street,
he didn't brake, he travelled down it faster.

He said, "I look at your life as a piece of work in progress origami.
It looks like shit right now but one day, it will be beautiful."
A joke
but I agreed.

He tells me to lean on him,
asks me what I need,
after speaking, thanks me for sharing
as though what I've said isn't out of self-indulgent greed.

When I speak to him
my words project back at me in his eyes.
He's trying to see what I see
so he can empathise.

He spoke to me like me
when I was impossible to recognise,
advised me not to hide in the darkness
reasoning fear can't find me beneath its disguise.

He speaks to me, about me, for me,
not to tell the other guys.
Never says "relax" or "calm down"
knowing it's not rational to feel those things all of the time.

When it first happened with him
and my emotions shifted into overdrive,
he held me while I cried and said,
"I wore a green t-shirt so you can snot on it all you like."

Every time since
when an episode does arise,
he takes a moment to change his shirt
so any brain matter doesn't have to be compromised.

When I panic he asks, "Shall we do some breathing?"
because it's not as simple as something I've been doing my whole life.
He gives me butterflies. Not ones that are about to take flight,
ones that aren't afraid to fight to survive.

"You owe me one," he'll jest
when he lends me art supplies
but, "Don't mention it,"
in return for a night of restraining me from knives.

"*You* go, *I* go!"
should never be a settlement to keep someone alive
but the thought of him going
is not one I can bear to bring to mind.

The way he spoke of his friends when we first met
was like each put a star in the night sky or were the reason for
        every sunset.
I remember wanting him to speak of me the same way,
vowing to become someone he would never forget.

At my lowest I put him up so high
it was hard to look at him without an ache in my neck.

He was my morphine.

I was mindful not to over-prescribe
to avoid an addiction that would add to the battle to survive.
I allowed myself to feel every emotion for him
to test out which ones were justified.

At his weakest he said, "I'm all in." He was bluffing.
This was not a hand he had strength in,
but I couldn't tell he had nothing
so he won the hand.

Then he took mine,
held it next to his and proved they are stronger together.
Assuring me a tear will never fall alone again
because his and mine are tethered.

He slept with lights on for me,
sacrificed his sleep so I could.
When I looked at him in horror because my mind told me he was
        a monster,
he didn't flinch, he pretended he understood.

Despite the tension,
sleep deprivation and nocturnal activity,
he maintained that I must be a genius
with a sleep pattern to mirror the likes of Emily Brontë or da Vinci.

When I lose who I am,
with silence he soothes me,
then he plays the songs in my heart
to recall my identity.

He confirmed I can survive on my own,
although blissfully unaware,
because when I believed his presence was set in stone, he had to go.
And I surfed a wave bigger than, in the past, I would have dared.

It was then I knew my life wouldn't be the same
without me.
Others are an honour
but I am the one I need.

He taught me lessons without ever having to preach.

"There must be something more" is the general consensus
but I fall for a human, not someone's gender.
If that's the rule my love life with friends would rival something
    from *Eastenders*.
You can feel this way without concealing a hidden agenda.

And I am in love with him!
In this unconditional friendship and acceptance of growth.
Lack of bitterness amid success,
lack of judgement throughout woe.

I like honesty.
And attention
but mainly honesty.
I can do it without him but with him, to a whole new degree.

For the foreseeable future
I'll line my wardrobe with t-shirts that are green.
If anyone needs a friend like him,
I'll try to be their true sense of security.

Finally, he said to me,
"You should hear what I say about you,"
and I knew I'd become the friend he talks about
like they are the most breath-taking view.

He's the last time I'll introduce myself
with, "Hi, I'm Jemima, I was abused."
He's not my knight in shining armour,
rather my anti-depressant in liquid form so it's easier to consume.

One day, he's going to meet someone who no stars or sunsets can
        out-do,
when he does, I'm going to fall in love with them too.
For showing him he is his everything
and that his flaws are the piece of his art which hold the most value.

These days, we hold each other's hearts in our hands when they're
        heavy,
then hold each other's hands for support.
He's been my composure during my storm and if my storm
        doesn't cease,
I hope to be flashes of light on his days when clouds show no remorse.

I took everything he said as gospel
and tried to sing along,
he still plays the melody some days
but now I sing the lyrics to my own song.

He's an anomaly I wish there were more of
but then he'd be two, three, forty in a million, not one.
His flaws aren't invisible but in a society of needing to be right,
he isn't afraid of getting things wrong.

When my roots were digging down
finding their way,
he was the whisper through the neighbouring trees reassuring me
I would be my own source of energy one day.

Now I take a gold dusted leaf out of his book
and keep it on display.
A reminder, words have the power to give a cliffhanger
less falling space.

If a trick of the mind can aid navigation rather than cause delay,
I want to be a magician.
And if you are someone's friend in the green t-shirt, wow.
You are giving "unconditional" its definition.

Let's hope that streetlight through yonder window breaks,
through my blinds and rests upon my face.
Illuminating the monster and transforming him into man,
alleviating doubt and fear with its ambient orange glow.
If only life could be so kind
to pour the glow into the mind behind the eyes
that have to close and submit to the treacherous, glow-less abyss.
The cruellest irony that we must plunge into our deepest doubt in order
to retain our sanity.
You carry with you an exuding glow of your own.
The girl who wears love on her sleeve and emotions on the ends
of her fingers.
It would be a lie to say that it is always easy,
but there is never a doubt as to whether it is worth it, for a day spent with
such a beautiful mind.
An hour of lucidity.
Or, a second where everything is yellow.

By: The friend in the green t-shirt.

ACKNOWLEDGEMENTS

Tim Horgan, thank you for the crack of dawn wake-up call and breath-taking (literally, it was freezing) photoshoot which created the cover for this book. Not to mention the contribution of your poem.

Clive and Nick, thank you for booking me to do my first head-liner in December 2018 at Oooh Beehive Swindon, and for the unbelievable support ever since.

Spoz, my ace and bostin' mentor and friend. Thank you for featuring a version of my poem "Tornado" in your book *Sometimes Angry* published with Verve Poetry Press.

Ryan, thank you for making sure I didn't have to go on any of the early road trips alone.

Scott and James, thank you for being a strong team.

Thank you to the much needed poetry scene which gives us the important opportunity to be heard.

Rick and Rob, thank you both for spending your patience on helping me through the editing process.

Stuart and Verve Poetry Press, you've given this book the freedom to be everything I imagined and so much more, I cannot thank you enough.

ABOUT VERVE POETRY PRESS

Verve Poetry Festival is a new press focussing initially on meeting a local need in Birmingham - a need for the vibrant poetry scene here in Brum to find a way to present itself to the poetry world via publication. Co-founded by Stuart Bartholomew and Amerah Saleh, it is publishing poets from all corners of the city - poets that represent the city's varied and energetic qualities and will communicate its many poetic stories.

Added to this is a colourful pamphlet series featuring poets who have previously performed at our sister festival - and a poetry show series which captures the magic of longer poetry performance pieces by poets such as Polarbear and Matt Abbott.

Like the festival, we strive to think about poetry in inclusive ways and embrace the multiplicity of approaches towards this glorious art.

www.vervepoetrypress.com
@VervePoetryPres
mail@vervepoetrypress.com